The Longest, Darkest Night!

The story of a Total Lunar Eclipse on Winter Solstice
as experienced by a community of animals

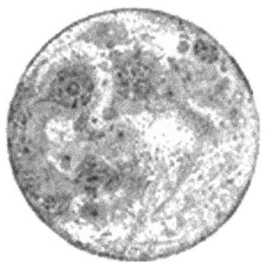

by

Peter B. Lewis

Illustrated by
Leslie W. LePere

Published by: AUDISEE MEDIA

A division of
Better Sound All Around, LLC
Seattle, WA 98101

© 2020 Peter B. Lewis
Second Edition
All Right Reserved
No part of this book may be reproduced or transmitted in any form or by any means, electronic or mechanical, including photocopying, recording or by any information storage and retrieval system, without written permission of the publisher.

For information contact Peter@AUDISEE.com

ISBN 978-0-9980365-6-4

Trademarks, AUDISEE and The Longest, Darkest Night! are registered in the USA and other countries.

Printed in the United States of America

For all grandchildren

Up North in winter, the days are short and the nights are long. The longest night is known as Winter Solstice, and often falls on December 21st. For the trees of the forest and the animals of the night, called nocturnal animals, Winter Solstice is a night of peace and sharing stories. Even the trees join in.

Grampa Cedar, the eldest, has the oldest story and he tells it slowly. "We are in for a special night tonight children," he says, "because tonight there will be a..."

All around, the snow and the land look weird. It's dark, dangerous, silent. Just then Grampa Cedar whispers on the wind. "This is the special night I'm telling you about. We are having a Total Eclipse of the Moon. This happens rarely. And the rarest of all is tonight, on Winter Solstice."

"What's an Eclipse?" Young Weasel asks and everyone wants to know.

"Well," Grandpa Cedar replies, "in tonight's Eclipse, the Earth in blocking the light of the sun so the Moon sits in the dark for a little while. There is no danger."

"You mean we're not doomed?" asks Young Weasel.

"No, my dear Weasel, as your friend Mr. Raccoon said, 'The Moon was full when she rose, and she'll be full again when she sets in the morning.'"

"I don't believe it," cries Brother Fox. "The light of the Moon has gone out and we are all done for!"

"Please be at ease, Brother Fox," Grampa Cedar continues. "Everything will soon be back to normal. Most of Earth's creatures are asleep, and won't even know it happened."

Madam Opossum asks,
"Are you sure?"

Grampa Cedar whispers,
"Wait a while longer little one, you'll see."

"Oh," says Mrs. Owl, "Winter Solstice and a total eclipse of the Moon? Why yes, I remember now, Great Grandfather Owl told us tales about it. He didn't see it himself mind you. Oh nooo-it was much too long ago. His great grandfather told him, and he told me. Hooot hooo, this is exciting!"

And then a reddish glow
comes over the Moon's face.

"We are in real trouble now!"
shouts Brother Fox as he stares
out into the forest. "Look! The Moon
is on fire and we're all going to get cooked!"

"We are so doomed!" sobs Young Weasel.

Again Grampa Cedar's voice is carried
on the wind. "The Moon is reflecting
the colors of all sunsets and sunrises
on Earth at this moment. Isn't it beautiful?
It's a special gift on the longest night of
the year."

Madam Opossum asks Grampa Cedar, "How did you know things would turn out OK?"

"Because I am the elder of this forest," Grampa Cedar says slowly. "I have lived many winters and seen many things. All that living has made me wise. It is my greatest strength and a valuable resource for our community."

"Yeah," says Young Weasel, "I've noticed things usually go better when we listen to our elders." Everyone agrees!

The animals are quiet as things return to normal. Then Mrs. Owl and Mr. Raccoon begin singing an ancient song about the importance of working together. Soon everyone is singing!

THE SONG OF SOLSTICE
(to the tune of "Frère Jacques")

Earth keeps turning, the World keeps turning, round and round, round and round. Love holds us together. Life is getting *[warmer?]*, turn around, turn around. (repeat)

After the song, Grampa Cedar speaks again. "I am proud of you my forest family. You are very brave! Even though you were afr‌ of the dark and unknown, your courage defeated your fears. Now we are on our way to brighter days ahead."
The trees russle their applause.

The Moon sets moments before first light. Tonight Winter Solstice has extra meaning, honoring the value of hope, celebrating family, especially our elders, lifting us all up to the brighter days ahead. Before the sun breaks the horizon, the nocturnal animals start for home. They all stop to thank Grampa Cedar for sharing his wisdom and helping them all enjoy the longest, darkest night!

The End

Scientific

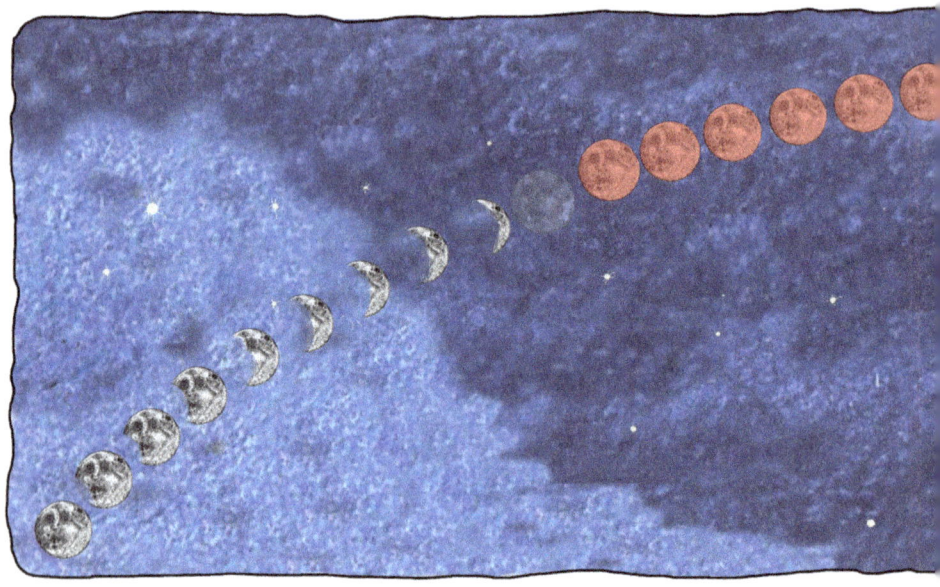

How far away is the moon?
While our Moon and Earth remain locked in orbit, the moon is very slowly inching away, at a rate of about 1.5 inches a year. Right now the moon is more than 238,000 miles from Earth, and when it formed, some models suggest it might have been as close as 14,000 miles.

How big is it?
The moon's diameter is 2,159.2 miles. Equatorial circumference is 6,783.5 miles. Surface area is about 14.6 million square miles, which is less than the total surface area of the continent of Asia, about 17.2 million square miles. Our moon is the brightest object in our sky. It appears quite large, because it is the nearest celestial body. The moon is a bit more than one-quarter (27%) the size of Earth.

A little-understood optical effect makes the moon look bigger on the horizon. This trick of the brain has been observed since ancient times. You can test whether it's just an illusion. At Moonrise, hold your thumb up next to the moon and compare the moon's size with your thumbnail. Later, when the moon is higher in the sky, look again!

Notes

Some Celestial Cycles

The Earth rotates on its axis, one rotation per day. The Moon rotates on its axis about one rotation per month and the Moon orbits Earth about once each month. The Earth and Moon orbit the Sun, once per year. Other planets orbit our Sun, and some have moons orbiting them. This makes up our solar system.

Astronomers have found more than 500 solar systems and discover new ones every year. Scientists estimate that there may be tens of billions of solar systems in our Milky Way galaxy, perhaps even as many as 100 billion. It has only been a few years since the first solar system outside of ours was detected!

Rarest of Events!

Geoff Chester of the US Naval Observatory inspected a list of eclipses going back 2000 years. "Since Year 1, I can only find one previous instance of an eclipse matching the same calendar date as the solstice, and that is 1638 DEC 21," says Chester. "Fortunately we won't have to wait 372 years for the next one...that will be on 2094 DEC 21."

The Moon is a cold, rocky orb. Similar to Earth, the Moon has no light of its own. It reflects sunshine from its surface. As the Moon orbits Earth, the changing position of the Moon with respect to the Sun, causes it to cycle through a series of phases. Many early civilizations used the phases of the Moon to measure the passage of time.

The word month is derived from moon.

Hebrew, Muslim and Chinese calendars are lunar calendars.
The New Moon phase is the beginning of the Moon's monthly cycle.

A Full Moon always rises at sunset, is visible all night and sets at sunrise. This is because the Moon is directly opposite the Sun in the sky when the Moon is full. None of the Moon's other phases have this unique characteristic.

Full   Gibbous   Third Quarter   Cresent

ere did the Moon come from?

Moon is thought to have formed about 4.51 billion years ago, when Earth was ially molten (melted rock) and the heavy iron had sunk into the core of the planet. most widely accepted explanation is that the Moon formed after a giant impact ween Earth and a Mars-sized body called Theia. A fraction of the debris formed g around Earth and, according to some computer models, in about a month's , aggregated into the moon. The moon is in the vacuum of space and has no osphere.

ar eclipse

ng a total lunar eclipse, the Earth blocks the Sun's light from the Moon. u were on the Moon you would see a Solar Eclipse, as the Earth completely ses the Sun. From the Moon, you would see a bright red ring around Earth, e sunrises and sunsets around the world! A total lunar eclipse is so interesting beautiful because of the filtering and refracting effect of Earth's atmosphere on rays of the Sun as they are reflected on the Moon's surface.

tal eclipse of the Moon only occurs during a Full Moon, when the Moon passes ugh Earth's shadow.

What is a nocturnal animal?

Nocturnal animals are more active at night and sleep during the day, often in a burrow or den. Many desert animals are nocturnal to escape extreme daytime heat.
Bats and owls avoid other winged competitors by hunting for food at night.
Many nocturnal animals also take advantage of the cover of darkness to avoid predators.
Nocturnal animals have special adaptations to survive in the dark.
For example, nighttime animals often have large eyes to see better in the dark.

Some nocturnal animals from around the world

- Aye-Aye
- Badger
- Bandicoot
- Bat
- Bat-eared fox
- Beaver
- Binturong
- Bilby
- Black rhinoceros
- Galago (bushbaby)
- Bush rat
- Capybara (some are crepuscular)
- Caracal
- Cat
- Catfish
- Chinchilla
- Civet
- Cockroach
- Cougar
- Coyote
- Cricket
- Cyprus spiny mouse
- Dingo
- Dwarf crocodile
- Eastern woolly lemur
- Firefly
- Flying squirrel
- Gerbil (some are diurnal)
- Great grey slug
- Hamster
- Hedgehog
- Hermit crab
- Honey badger
- Hyena
- Hoffmann's two-toed sloth
- Iranian jerboa
- Jaguar (bordering on crepuscular)
- Kangaroo (most)
- Koala (mostly nocturnal)
- Kinkajou
- Kit fox (mostly nocturnal)
- Leopard
- Leopard gecko
- Lion (bordering on crepuscular)
- Margay
- Mink (bordering on crepuscular)
- Mouse
- Nine-banded armadillo
- Octodon (rodents) (degus species diurnal)
- Oncilla
- Ocelot
- Opossum
- Owl
- Panamanian night monkey
- Pangolin
- Paradoxical frog
- Porcupine
- Possum
- Python regius
- Quoll
- Rabbit rat
- Raccoon
- Red-eyed tree frog
- Red fox
- Scorpion
- Skunk
- Slow loris
- Spectacled bear
- Sportive lemur
- Sugar glider
- Tapeti
- Tarantula
- Tarsier
- Tasmanian Devil
- Tiger (most species)
- Onychophora (velvet worms)
- Western woolly lemur
- White-faced storm petrel (when caring for young)
- White-tailed deer (bordering on crepuscular)
- Wombat

Crepuscular means active in twilight.
Diurnal means active during the day.

About Cedar:
The Western Red Cedar provided a wealth of raw materials vital to the early Northwest Coast Indians and their art and culture. Known as the "Tree of Life," native people used its wood for housing, canoes and carvings; its soft inner bark for clothing, blankets and baskets; its branches for rope, incense and medicine; and its roots for basketry. Nothing was wasted.

About Fox:
Red foxes are the largest true fox. Their fur grows longer and thicker in winter. Instead of sleeping in a den, an adult fox will sleep curled up on the open ground, with its fluffy tail over its nose and feet to protect itself from the cold. The Arctic fox is well adapted to living in cold environments. It has a deep thick fur which is brown in summer and white in winter.

About Opossum:
Opossums are marsupials (mammals with a pouch in which they carry their young), a primitive group of mammals. Opossums lived during the time of the dinosaurs and one reason for their continued survival is their ability to eat nearly anything. Very often opossums will alter their foraging habits during winter, coming out during the day when it is warmer rather than at night.

About Owl:
Owls have wide wings, lightweight bodies and feathers specially designed to allow them to silently swoop down. Adult owls hoot, screech or whistle. Owls live in dense forests, open woodlands, deserts and urban environments. Snowy owls have keen eyesight and great hearing, which can help them find prey that is hidden under thick vegetation or snow-cover. Owls deftly snatch their quarry with their sharp talons.

About Raccoon:
Winter a challenging time for most animals in the forest. Raccoons are extremely adaptable and stay warm and fed through the winter months. Raccoons are omnivores, and will take advantage of any local food source. They grow thick warm coats and find cozy warm dens to sleep in.

About Weasel:
Weasel changes color seasonally for protection: snowy white in winter, brown in summer. The long-tailed weasel is a fearless and aggressive hunter, which may attack animals far larger than itself. When stalking, it waves its head from side-to-side in order to pick up the scent of its prey.

Books about the Moon by other authors

Jude's Moon. Guettier, Nancy. New York: Henry Holt and Company. 2014. Jude loves the moon so much it becomes his best friend. Then one day the moon is no longer round, it's shaped like a croissant. Join Jude and his brother who teaches him what the real names are for the phases of the moon and why they occur.

Keepers of the Night: Native American Stories and Nocturnal Activities for Children. Bruchac, Joseph and Michael J. Daduto. Golden, CO: Fulcrum Books. 1994. Native American sky stories, including ones about the Moon, lunar and solar eclipses, and day and night are accompanied by activities.

The Kids Book of the Night Sky. Love, Ann and Jane Drake. Toronto, Ontario: 2004. Learn about the secrets of the night sky, throughout the seasons. Play games, keep a star log like an astronomer, read about night sky myths and how to read a star map.

Margaret and the Moon: How Margaret Hamilton Saved the First Lunar Landing. Robbins, Dean. New York: Knopf Books for Young Readers. 2017. Learn how scientist Margaret Hamilton used her childhood love of mathematics to help NASA put a man on the moon. Without her handwritten computer code, NASA's Apollos 8 through 11 might still be on the launching pad!

Moon! Earth's Best Friend (Our Universe Book 3). McAnulty, Stacy. New York: Henry Holt and Company. 2018. In this fun picture book, the moon herself tells the story of how she was formed. Moon will never turn away from her best friend Earth. They'll always be there for each other.

The Birth of the Moon. Coby Hol, 2000, North South Books. In this illustrated recreation of a Native American tale, the Sun gives the Moon as a gift to the animals so they can see at night, and makes the Moon wax and wane to remind them to appreciate the gift. Ages 3 – 6.

Moontellers: Myths of the Moon from Around the World. Lynn Moroney, 1995, Northland Publishing Company
Colorfully illustrated stories from indigenous tribes around the world will engage readers 9 -13 and parents will enjoy reading to younger children.

My notes and observations

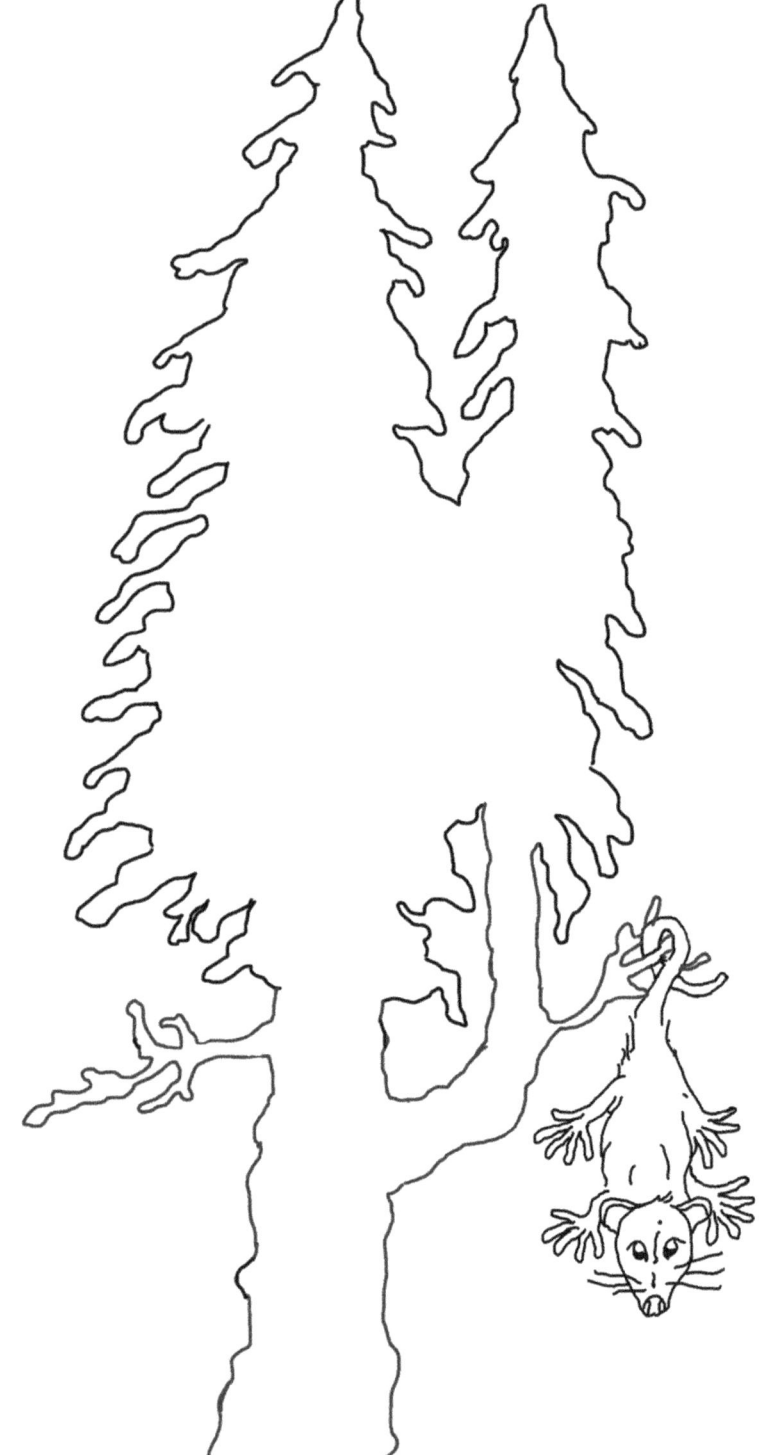

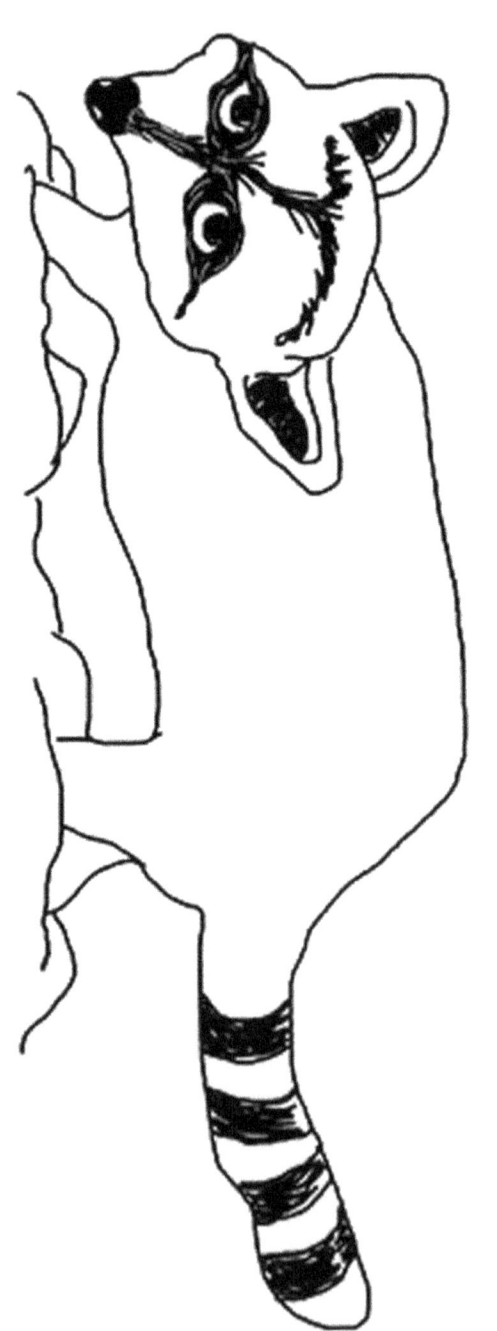

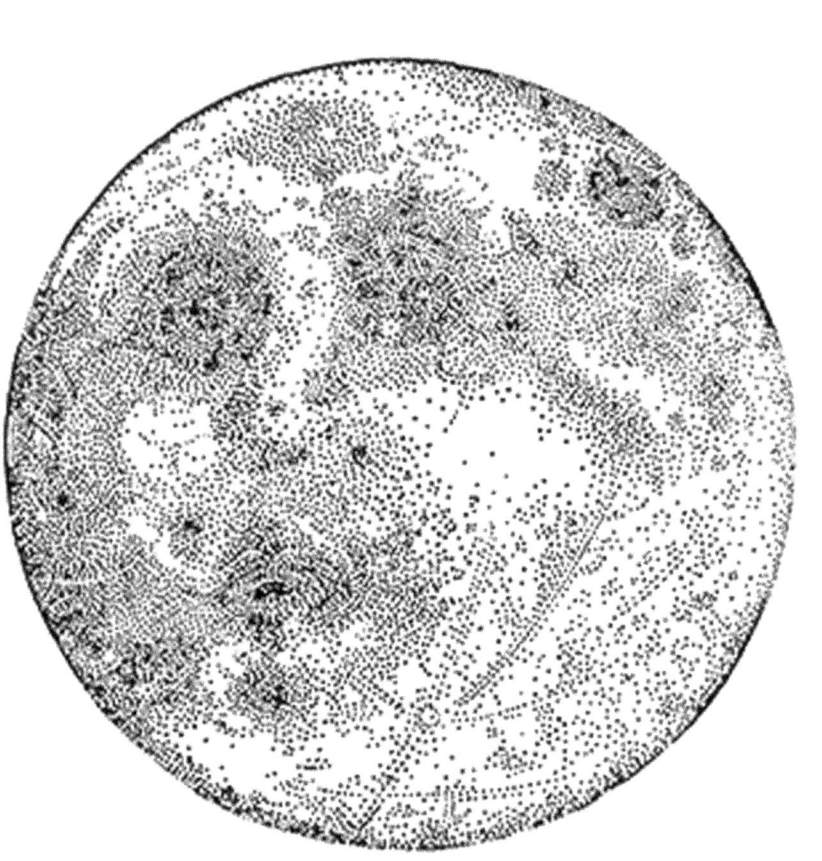

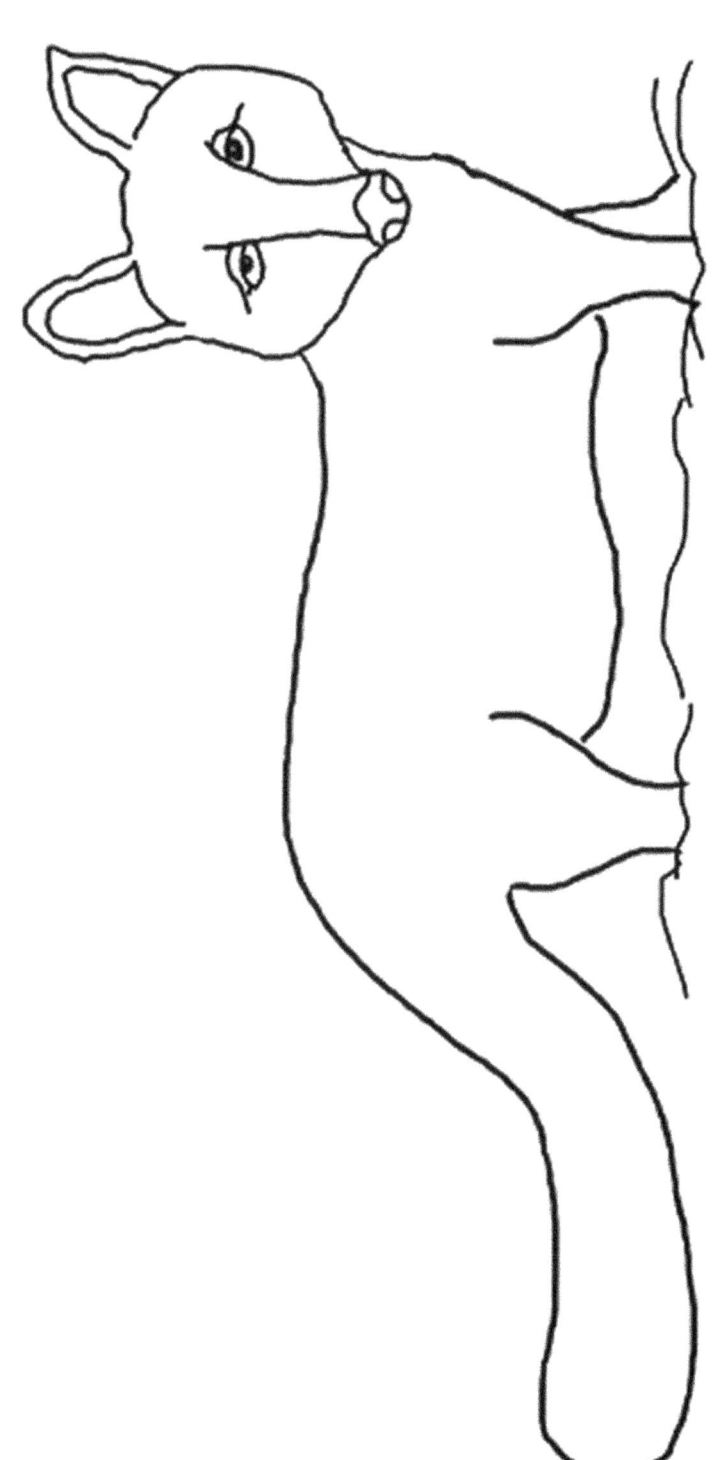

Acknowledgements

The Longest, Darkest Night! began as a story to be performed on stage. I am so grateful to all who helped make this story into the beautiful book you now hold.

　Claire Meeker
　Ralph Miller
　Jennifer McCord
　Marcia Pettersen and the 3rd Grade Teachers
　Marletta Iwasyk
　Marti Kaplan
　Samantha and Judy Lewis
　Alain Brion
　Tim Huling for the music
　Caroline Goodell
　Cherie Seymore
　Pat Cashman
　Gary Crow
　Mo Rivers
　David Levy
　Frank Sandborn
　Marvin and Judy Lieberman
　Terry Small and Bill Bruning
　Debra Bouchegnies
　Luanne Brown

Electronic Graphic Wizard, Chemyn Kodis
Thank you for your prolific skills and patience.

And an extra special thank you to Leslie W. LePere who brought the story to life with his enthusiasm and fanciful illustrations.

If you enjoyed *The Longest, Darkest Night!*, please visit www.PeterBLewis.com for more information and events.

I was given this story by the wonderful farm cat Cali, when I lived on 20 acres off of Lake Joy Road. She was responsible for keeping the vermin population under control and she did her job skillfully for many years. Cali loved the stalking, the chase and the inevitable end.

After a time however, she preferred to lay by the fire in winter and share tales of what was and what might have been.

We both hope you enjoy this one!

Photo by Kevin Costello

www.ingramcontent.com/pod-product-compliance
Lightning Source LLC
Chambersburg PA
CBHW051603010526
44118CB00023B/2808